Build Business Credit the Fastest Way Possible

by
Garry Pompee

Garry Pompee

Dedications

I dedicate this book to my maker, my Lord and Savior Jesus Christ, for allowing me to share my experiences. Also, to the best mother EVER, Rose Marie Pompee! My first-born son, Ian Prince Pompee and my nephew Dishon Smith, I do "this" for them. To my sister, Fabianne Pompee and brother Harold Pompee Lastly, I save the best for last to my best friend who always supported me throughout the whole book process and greatest mother of my child and wife Nefertiti Pompee. Without you I wouldn't be the man I am today, I will always love you.

Garry Pompee

Disclaimer

Disclosure

The information and materials contained herein are for YOU OR YOUR CORPORATION ONLY and is based upon the opinion of the Author, Garry Pompee Owner of Prestige Elite Group. It Should not be construed as legal or financial advice. Be sure to consult an Attorney or CPA on any legal or financial matters.

* Please Note: Processing times to complete the corporation set-up is 1-2 months depending upon the workload of your state office. You will establish the entity: C CORP, S CORP, LLC, NONPROFIT--- according to the rules and regulations of "your state" in which the business is located. Every step after that will be the same statewide when it comes to building business credit. Please read through each form for complete understanding before signing

Table of Contents

Acknowledgement

This work would not have been possible without the support of Prestige Elite Group and the Business Financial Suite. I am especially grateful for all my success with my business ventures and to my mother Rose Pompee who worked 3 jobs to take care of her 3 kids and to my wonderful caring beautiful wife, Nefertiti Pompee for always having my back and staying up late night with me at 5 am to read any errors in spelling and ideas for this book. You have been supportive of my career goals and worked actively to provide for our first-born son Ian Prince Pompee. I am grateful to all of those with whom I have had the pleasure to work with during this and other related projects. I would especially like to thank Ty Crandall from Credit Suite for all your YouTube videos about Business Credit. You taught me more than I could ever give you credit for here. He has shown me, by his example, what a good teacher (and person) should be. Nobody has been more important to me in the pursuit of this project than the members of my family.

30 Days 50K is my heart and that is what I pour out to the readers. I hope you take what you learn from my book and use it to build your business credit like it helped my corporation and you also receive the funding you need to grow your business. Peace out and Enjoy your reading.

Chapter 1

Corporation Setup

CORPORATION TYPES

When you're on the path to building business credit, I've learned there's 3 types of entities that are important.

- C Corporation. A corporation is a separate legal entity set up under state law that protects owner (shareholder) assets from creditor claims. Incorporating your business automatically makes you a regular, or "C" corporation. A C corporation (or C Corp) is a separate taxpayer, with income and expenses taxed to the corporation and not owners. ****Note: You will get more funding if your business is a C corp.**

- S Corporation. Once you've incorporated, you can elect S corporation status by filing a form with the IRS and with your state, if applicable, so that profits, losses and other tax items pass through the corporation to you and are reported on your personal tax return (the S corporation does not pay tax).

- Limited Liability Company (LLC). Another business type that is formed under state law and gives you personal liability protection is the LLC. Tax-wise, an LLC is similar to an S corporation (or S Corp), with business income and expenses reported on your personal tax return. If you are the only owner of an LLC, you are viewed as a "disregarded" entity. This means you report the LLC's income and expenses on Schedule C of Form 1040—the same schedule used by sole proprietors.

1

CORPORATION NAME

When you are starting a brand, you MUST always make sure nobody else is using your logo. The same thing applies with your business name.

Conduct a business name search within the U.S.A. by visiting: **https://www.legalzoom.com/business/business-formation/entity-name-check-overview.html**

Conduct a business name search International by visiting: **https://www.start.biz/business_names/search**

Please check with your state's city (registrar-recorder/county clerk) website.

You may search and view the names indexed to registrar recorder/county clerk, which expire 5 years from the date filed in the office of the County Clerk.

- **Searches on this system are inaccurate at times and a business name that you select may be an active business name. Please visit the recorder office for a more detailed search in your state/city.**

Perform a search on Google / Yahoo - simply type in the business name you would like to select. Do not use your own name within the name of your corporation. Do not be specific about the type of business in which the corporation will be engaged.

Be as generic and non-specific as possible, see the following:
- **Examples: PEG Corporation / First Jump Enterprise / 2-Top Diversified / OUI Corporation.**

CORPORATION IMAGE

Have you heard the saying "if it talks like a duck or walks like a duck, then most likely it's a duck," well that's what I will teach you in establishing a corporate image. The key is to look like you're a fortune 500 company.

- **Do NOT use PO BOXES.**

Get a professional business address. I recommend a virtual office, if you are a startup.
- **Recommended: regus.com or davincivirtual.com**

Use an 800 #. Set-up a professional voicemail message.
- **Recommended: ringcentral.com or freedomvoice.com**

Order professional stationary.
- **Recommended: vistaprint.com or overnightprints.com**

Build a Business Website.
- **Recommended: wix.com or us.webnode.com**

Your website does not have to be elaborate and expensive. Set-up a generic website with the following information:

You must have a: www.yourcorporation.com
HOME: Welcome to YOUR CORPORATION NAME.
ABOUT US: Enter about 3 paragraphs about your business
SERVICES: List your services
CAREERS: List your openings (even if you don't have an opening at the moment list your projected future openings)
CONTACT US: List your address (must match your credit files)
List your business email and business phone number.

Get a Business Domain for $1 at 1and1.com or godaddy.com with an added professional corporate email address.
- **Example: support@PEGCorporation.com**

3

**Remember to create the look and feel of a Fortune 500 Company.

- **Example: (website, business location, corporate email, social presence, etc.) Sample Address: Just Us Papers Corp. 123 West Lane, Suite 129 Any City, Any State, Zip Code**

EMPLOYER IDENTIFICATION NUMBER (EIN)

Your Tax ID number or the commonly used name EIN will be the number that identifies your business and information. It's just like how your social security number will identify who you are for personal credit.

You can get your EIN online instant on the IRS website Free:

- **Visit: irs.gov/businesses/small-businesses-self-employed/apply-for-an-employer-identification-number-ein-online**

Make sure the Business Name and Business Address (DO NOT USE YOUR HOME ADDRESS) that you apply with is the same information you will use in your business credit building.

go to page 3 for more details about acceptable addresses.

**Please note: You will establish the entity: C CORP, S CORP, LLC, NONPROFIT--- according to the rules and regulations of "your state" in which the business is located.

CONDUCTING BUSINESS UNDER A DBA

A DBA filing (doing business as, also called an assumed or fictitious business name) allows a company to transact business using a different name. It generally takes place at the county level, but some states have state-level DBA filings.

For sole proprietorships and general partnerships, unless a DBA is filed, the company name is the same as the owner's or owners' name(s). For example, Peter Smith is operating a landscaping business as a sole proprietorship. In order to transact business as Smith's Landscaping, he must file a DBA for that name. Otherwise, he must transact business as Peter Smith.

A corporation or LLC can also file a DBA to transact business under a name different from the one registered with the state (when the business was incorporated). For example, a corporation formed as Smith and Sons, Inc. may want to do business under a name that more clearly states what the company does and could file a DBA to use a more descriptive name like Smith Landscaping.

- **Please select and establish your business entity: C CORP, S CORP, LLC, NONPROFIT---according to the rules and regulations of "your state" in which the business is located.**

ADDING DIVISIONS TO CORPORATION

In the initial corporation set-up, divisions are not needed. You can always add them later under the corporation/entity.

A company may create multiple business divisions in order to market different products and services. Some companies form divisions based on the types of products or services, geographic location or demographic market sectors.

Corporations often form separate business divisions as a way to develop a competitive market advantage. Adding a division allows a company to expand without significantly modifying the company's existing corporate structure.

Divisions offer many opportunities. They are particularly crucial in protecting assets and lessening the burden of liability. Establish a division for each purpose and function of the corporation/entity.

You can have a sales division, marketing/research division, or a printing division. This strategy will allow you to buy many goods and services at wholesale prices and corporate rates. You should consider setting up at least three additional divisions.

Chapter 2

Articles of Incorporation

State Business Registration

Begin the process of registering your business with the state you plan to do business in by completing the Articles of Incorporation.

- **Recommended: incforfree.com (This is a Free service. Only pay for your State Fee.)**

Keep all documents in your corporate stock kit for referencing.
**Note: Processing times to receive your certified articles within a week depending upon the workload of your state office processing time may vary.

You may choose to have a registered agent for your business. A registered agent is the person who will receive any legal documents issued to the corporation. You can use yourself as an agent, but you have to be reachable at your location to receive Any mail or Legal Documents, if you are being served.

- **Recommended Registered Agent: freeregisteredagent.com**

Please Note: P.O BOXES CANNOT BE USED.

Make sure all information about your business matches the details you choose from (page 3– Corporation Image) before submitting your application with the state. If information doesn't match your Articles of Incorporation, when Applying for business credit than your application WILL get denied!

Please take the time to set up the entity correctly without skipping steps. Only skip if directed to do so but go back to your starting point and continue.

Ok to skip ahead if you have a step implemented already.

STATEMENT OF INFORMATION

You MUST complete your business SOI within the first 90 days of filing and receiving your charter # for Articles of Incorporation.

Instructions will be sent to you from the state. Please make sure you respond to all correspondence sent to you regarding the corporation/entity.

Make sure you complete this form each year to avoid the corporation from becoming inactive.

Review the rules and regulations of "your state" in which the business is located.

Your registered agent listed on your Article of Incorporation job is to forward all pertinent information to you regarding the corporation/entity.

- **Remember failure to complete this form will cause the corporation/entity to become inactive which will stop your business credit building efforts.**

SEAL & STOCK CERTIFICATE

When you receive your Articles of Incorporation back from the state you may proceed with ordering your corporate seal and stock certificates.

- **Recommended for Corporate Seal:
corpkit.com/Electronic-Corporate-Seal**

- **Recommended for Corporate Certificates:
corpkit.com/Corporate-kits-seals-certificates/Stock-Certificates-LLC-Shares-Certificates.html**

When getting your Seal & Stock Certificate:
Provide name of your corporation.
Provide state of your corporation.
Provide year corporation was incorporated.
Select for Profit Corporation.
Total number of authorized Shares: 75,000
Designation: COMMON STOCK

For-Profit Corporations, please provide the following share and par value information, as contained in your articles or certificate of incorporation:

- **Select: LEAVE BLANK**

You might be asking yourself why a company would issue shares with no par value. Do this because it helps you avoid liability to stockholders should the stock price take a turn for the worse.

- **For example, if a stock was trading at $5 per share and the par value on the stock was $10, theoretically, the company would have a $5-per-share liability.**

Par value has no relation to the market value of a stock. A no-par-value stock can still trade for tens or hundreds of dollars. It all

9

depends on what the market feels the company is worth. Processing time for your Stock Kit is 3-4 weeks. Your stock kit runs the corporation. You can order a stock kit from any company online. Edit the above as you see fit for the entity you are establishing.

Chapter 3

Business Visibility

411 LISTING

Vendors, lenders and banks will do their due diligence prior to extending business credit to the corporation. Don't expect to receive credit by skipping these key fundamental steps. Make sure your voicemail is set-up to answer in the exact name of the corporation.

Call your local phone provider and tell them you would like to obtain a business line (not a landline)

Ask them to remote call forward that number to your cell phone or home phone. Make sure your new business number has the same area code as the city your corporation is located, if you are using a local number.

- **Recommended you use an 800 # instead, or both.**

Make sure you have your corporate Article of Incorporation and EIN on hand. Some companies may ask for this information. Also have your representative lists your corporation's physical address and phone number with 411 while they are setting up your account. Complete corporate conformity (411 listing, verifications, business license, etc.) –must be ACCURATE.

- Recommended for listing on 411:
  listyourself.net/ListYourself
- Recommended for listing in Multiple Directory:
  1and1.com/local-business-listings

BUSINESS LICENSE

Getting a business license may or may not be necessary depending on your business type or your state's licensing regulations.

I found out that most states don't have a comprehensive business licensing search website. Some do (such as New York and Oregon), others have a "one-stop" business registration website that includes permitting and licenses, and still others have a dedicated page directing business owners to contact their local town or city clerk for business licensing information.

- **Here's a compile list of Business Licensing Resources by State to get you going in the right direction:**
  nav.com/blog/266-business-licensing-by-state-5008

Contact the following departments in your city/state and find out what they require when obtaining a business license:

- **Business Tax, Registration, and Licenses Permits, Licenses, and Inspections**

BUSINESS BANK ACCOUNT

Apply at a physical bank that you see fit for your business with access to a bank business specialist, an online bank is fine if it meets the criteria for your business but for your convince a walk-in bank best fits your business.

Make sure your bank has the option to provide your business with services like Payroll, Merchant Services, Business Credit Cards, Business Loans and Business Line of Credit and more.

Contact the following banks and be prepared to give copies of the following information:

Resolution to open a bank account (sample located inside your corporate stock kit).

- **Note: Make sure you put your corporation seal on the resolution.**

Articles of Incorporation •Officers List (If more than one Owner of corporation) • EIN # • $50-$100 to deposit into the account.

The above may vary from state to state.

The two banks listed below provide great services to new corporations. You may select a different bank based on the corporation/entity needs.

- **Recommended Banks: USBank.com and WellsFargo.com**

If you have a business checking account set up already have the bank associate link this account with the new corporation account.

This gives you history between the two accounts.

Apply for the first set of credit card(s) for the corporation/entity.

You will do all of this on your first visit to the bank. This is optional. Apply when you are ready!

At any given time, be prepared to provide a personal guarantee (meaning your SSN) for the business credit lines, "revolving accounts". If you don't want to provide it or have personal credit issues, use a Credit Profile Number instead, also known as CPN to Apply for Business Credit Cards. But remember it is always better to fix your issues on your SSN.

- **Visit page 17 for more information about CPN.**

PLEASE- select and use ONE BANK ONLY. Multiple banks are not necessary.

13

Chapter 4

Vendor Accounts (Net-30)

One of the easiest ways to start off on the right foot when it comes to business credit is to get net-30 accounts with companies that report to commercial credit agencies.

But what is a net-30 account?

A net-30 account is one that extends you 30 days to pay the bill in full after you have purchased products or services.

So what other accounts are out there?

Here's a simple way to get started if your business is young, or your business isn't making a lot of money yet: vendor credit.

Vendor credit is when you purchase goods or services from vendors that allow you to buy now and pay later. Vendor credit is not just limited to net-30 accounts either—some vendors offer net-15 (15 days to pay), net-60, or even net-90 day terms.

Vendors that then report those payments to commercial credit agencies are the ones that will help your company establish business credit.

Always have the following with you when setting up accounts:
- **Resolution to open a vendor account, Articles of Incorporation, Corporate Charter #, Officers List and EIN #**

If a vendor asks for SSN tell them, you only want to set up a business account. If they persist, tell them no thank you, hang up and call back in a day to speak with another representative.

Remember you can access these vendors by calling, faxing, or order directly from their websites. Always look for the commercial/business section.

- **Jedi Trick: On corporate letterhead, place your order listing the items you want. Make sure to include product numbers. Make it look like a Fortune 500 invoice – this method always gets approval.**

Some vendors will require a SSN regardless - you determine if this is the route you want to take. If your personal score is not up to par - use a CPN. (Covered later on page 17) You can add as many vendors as you like it's totally up to the goals of the corporation/entity.

- **Recommended Top 4 Vendors: Uline.com, Reliable.com (now merged with office depot) Quill.com & Grainger.com**

Access the vendors websites. If you registered already simply log in using your password and username. Place your first orders with the vendors listed above. Order in the amount of $150.00. You want to repeat this for up to 4-5 months. This is to develop payment history with the credit agencies. The goal is an 80 Paydex.

**You can place continuous orders with the above and achieve your 80 paydex goal. When you achieve 80 move on to the next set of vendors. Place the same amount $150 at the second level of vendors if you choose to add more vendors. Once at an 80 paydex, start completing revolving credit applications. Anything below $100.00 amount will not report and your

efforts will be a waste of time on vendor accounts. Order from all 4 vendors at the same time or order individually.

Pay invoices ahead of the due date – you can increase your paydex score to 90 or higher by simply paying your invoices 10-20 days ahead of the due date. A big plus on your files!

Build solid payment history – while account types and trade lines are a factor keep in mind that a payment track record is the final ingredient. Don't think that one paid invoice will make your business capable of acquiring no personal guarantee credit lines or credit cards. This is a continuous process

Second Level of Vendors (Establish Corporate Accounts): Kinkos, Staples, Target Commercial, Amazon, Sam's Club, Home Depot, Lowes, Shell and other gas stations, Verizon, Walmart, Sprint and other phone services, Dell Computers, Seton, Sheraton, Marriott, Hyatt, Apple, Best Buy, Costco, FedEx, UPS, Mercedes, Ford, GMC, Toyota, BMW and Ace Hardware

As you go through this process you will add to the list of vendors.

- ****WARNING-- Do not go on an application spree. This will RED FLAG your corporation/entity for sure! Once the corporation/entity is RED FLAGGED - you will not be able to do anything. You will have to start all over again - establishing a new corporation.**

Establish a minimum of "5"accounts. Establish bank credit with your small business bank account. Obtain secured business credit cards. Open a small business credit line. Establish a diversity of credit – build a strong business credit rating by obtaining different account types. This includes trade credit, revolving credit, loans and leases. Keep proper financials and maintain your stock kit.

Chapter 5

Personal Credit Issues

CREDIT PROFILE NUMBER (CPN)

A CPN is a nine-digit number that has the exact same genetic makeup of a Social Security Number (SSN). It is simply an available file number at the credit bureaus that can have financial information and payments reported.

You have the right to establish this number only once, so do not abuse it. This explanation is not here to advise anyone to misrepresent your Social Security Number, as you are completely responsible for any debts you incur using your CPN.

CPN's are used by celebrities, congress members/government workers, and witness protection reasons. It is your legal right to keep your Social Security Number private and use a separate number for any credit related purposes.

- **Note: You are only required by law to disclose your Social Security Number to the Internal Revenue Service (IRS), your employer, when registering a motor vehicle, buying a firearm, or applying and obtaining a federally-insured loan such as FHA, Sallie Mae, etc.**

If you're interested in obtaining a CPN number, you will have to find a company that sells these numbers. There are many companies that offer CPN numbers.

- **Recommended CPN provider: BusinessFinancialSuite.com**

Above all else, you need to be cautious about who you get a CPN number from. Make sure you know what you are paying for. You don't want to get a number that will cause problems for you. Find a legitimate company that has been selling CPN numbers online for a long time. If you work with someone like this, you shouldn't have any issues.

For a CPN number you will need to provide your Name, D.O.B and an address you have never used before. The address is the most important thing because if you use a current home address you run the risk of your CPN merging with credit established on your SSN file. ID, Email, telephone and employment information is optional.

**PAY ATTENTION TO DETAIL - YOU MUST FOLLOW ALL INSTRUCTIONS TO SET UP YOUR CPN CALLED "TRI-MERGED" – THERES OPTIONS TO PURCHASE A CPN THAT IS ALREADY TRI-MERGED MEANING SET UP FOR YOU AT 3 CREDIT BUREAU AND PUBLIC DIRECTORIES LISTED.

1. If you do not have a phone - Please go to Textnow.com and get one.
2. Go to Listyourself.net and do the 411 directory with your CPN profile.
3. Go to https://www.optoutprescreen.com and OPT-IN for pre-screened offers for credit cards.
4. Go to CapitalOne.com and do the Venture card for excellent credit.
5. Go to Barclays cards and do World Elite card for excellent credit.
6. Both cards above will be DENIED. (We are just establishing your CPN profile.)
7. Go to DriveTime.com and get your approval.
8. Go to MDG.com and get your approval.

Go to Creditreport.com and open up your monitoring with your CPN profile. If you cannot open it up, then it means you DID NOT follow instructions 1 through 8.

**Note: WAIT 10 business days before you do anything else with your CPN profile. DO NOT SKIP THIS PART AT ALL! It's very IMPORTANT!

MAKE YOUR PUBLIC RECORDS STRONGER FOR YOUR CPN WITH A STRONG ESTABLISHED PROFILE ON PUBLIC DIRECTORIES.

Please do as many of these reward/loyalty cards as you can:

- TV GUIDE: http://www.tvguide.com/

- SPIRIT REWARDS: https://www.spirit.com/freespiritlogin.aspx

- DELTA REWARDS: http://www.delta.com/content/www/en_US/skymiles/manage-my-account.htmww

- UNITED REWARDS: https://www.united.com/web/en-US/apps/account/account.aspx

- JC PENNY REWARDS: https://www.jcprewards.com/

- FUEL REWARDS: https://www.fuelrewards.com/login-signup.html

- MY POINT REWARDS: https://www.mypoints.com/emp/u/index.vm

- SAFEWAY REWARDS:
  https://www.safeway.com/ShopStores/OSSO-
  Login.page?goto=http%3A%2F%2Fwww.safeway.com%3
  A80%2FShopStores%2FMyCard.page

- WALGREENS BALANCE REWARDS:
  https://www.walgreens.com/balancerewards/balance-
  rewards.jsp

- MARRIOTT REWARDS:
  https://www.marriott.com/signIn.mi

- SEARS REWARDS:
  http://www.sears.com/search=my%20rewards%20points%
  20balance

- AUTO ZONE REWARDS:
  https://www.autozonerewards.com/viewLogin.htm

- ACE HARDWARE REWARDS:
  https://www.acehardware.com/acerewards/index.jsp?ste

Once you are done with the reward / loyalty cards, do the
following:

1. Sign up for all social media sites using your CPN profile
   information (Facebook, Twitter, Instagram, Google+, etc.).
2. Sign up for all major emails: (Gmail, Yahoo, AOL,
   Outlook, Protonmail, etc.).
3. Sign up for FREE magazines.
4. Sign up for YouTube and Spotify
5. Sign up for numerous monitoring sites that are free
   (Quizzle.com - CreditKarma.com - FreeCreditReport.com -
   Etc.)

If you are serious about your CPN you will follow all instructions. The more public records you do, the stronger it will become and the easier it will be for you to build it.

Note: I suggest using your CPN for 1 year until you received the funding your business needs and you fixed your SSN to 700 and Up. Because the goal is to use the CPN to get funding to grow your business and fix your SSN back in top shape. So, once you receive the funding you need to grow your business, what you do next is using that same CPN you established in top shape and then add your SSN as an Authorized User from tradelines you established with your CPN.

**MAKE SURE YOUR SSN INFORMATION DON'T MATCH YOUR CPN, WHEN ADDING AS AN AUTHORIZED USER (ex. Address, Phone, email, job)

The key is to make sure No information for your New CPN file links to your SSN.

- **Note: Use a virtual address that forwards to your home or ask a friend to use their home for mail. To use your virtual address, go to your local USPS Store and ask them to forward your mail temporarily for 6 months to your virtual address. So, basically your mail will get forwarded twice.**

- **Use a virtual number that forwards to your phone.**

- **Use a New email address you created from a different ip address, don't use your internet provider to open a New email address.**

- **Change your address on your ID. If, Not don't use it when applying for anything.**

21

**ALWAYS WAIT 30 DAYS BEFORE APPLYING FOR ANY TRADELINES FOR YOUR CPN OR SSN!

To generate a credit score you can go out and obtain a secured credit card and start establishing your own credit or add authorized user tradelines which are lines of credit that you piggyback onto your file to generate a credit score.

Now that you have established a strong public record it's time to get a score for your CPN by adding Tradelines or Build Out File.

Add an Authorized User Card either 1 or 2 preferably over 2 years old and over $2500 limits
less than 30% utilization to your CPN either from a family member/friend or purchase. Wait two
weeks after statement date for AU's to post.

**AFTER AU'S POST (OPTIONAL) you can add installment lines, auto lines, mortgage lines to your CPN, it's not necessary but a plus.

Once your AUs are posted to your file. Get yourself primary tradelines that I will explain to you later on Page 25.

REMEMBER, IT IS ALWAYS BETTER TO FIX YOUR SSN. OBTAINING A CPN IS ONLY AN ALTERNATIVE SOLUTION. EVEN THOUGH YOUR SSN SCORE IS NOT ABOVE 700, YOU CAN GET IT THERE SOONER BY ADDING AUTHORIZED USERS AND AGED TRADELINES.

You may need documents for verification when getting a car loan or house/Apt when using a CPN like ID, Paystubs, Utility bill, CPN card, W2. There're businesses that provide you with copies of documentations.
- **Recommended: BusinessFinancialSuite.com**

AUTHORIZED USERS TRADELINES

Adding a Tradeline (or sometimes called authorized user) is a way to improve your credit score. It can increase your chances to get higher "funding," qualifying for a house, an auto loan or whatever your credit goal is.

So, what exactly is an "Authorized User?"

An Authorized Users is someone who holds a credit line but is not the actual primary account holder.

- **Here's an example:**
  Say you are married, and you own a credit card with a $10,000 limit with a $500 balance. You add your wife with no credit history as an "Authorized User" with your credit card company so she can use your credit card etc. Now your past credit card history will show up on her credit as well just as it is on yours.

- **Remember, if the account holder defaults on payments than it will affect your score as well. Make sure you use a responsible account holder that keeps up with payments. You also won't have access to the primary account holder information or be able to use their credit card unless you know them, and they give it to you.**

How can the authorized user improve your credit?

Well, in the above example, the wife didn't have much credit at all, but her goal is to try to qualify for loans or credit cards in the future on her own. Since she has no credit, adding the authorized user will actually benefit the wife. The $10,000 limit will show up on her credit report now. This process is also called "piggybacking."

There is a misconception that adding authorized users to one's file will automatically make the credit skyrocket with super powers and now you qualify for $150,000 in loans etc.

Don't get me wrong, they do help or give a credit boost, but you must be somewhat realistic, they're not magic! Of course, banks can tell if an account is an authorized user or if it is actually your account (primary account) so keep that in mind.

BUT it does increase your credit score and improve history in the above example because she didn't have much credit history. Since the husband only owes $500, this low balance is a great low utilization. Banks will now see her credit report which will show the $10,000 credit card and be more prone to extending her credit now or approving her loan.

On the contrary, if the husband owed $10,000 then the credit card would be considered maxed out. If her goal was to try to get "funding," even though the husband has not missed one payment, it would hurt her credit since the balance or utilization is so high. Banks see this as being "maxed out" so they most likely would not like to extend her credit or approve her for a loan.

Revolving and installment accounts are 30% of your credit score so depending on how many accounts you have; an authorized user can greatly improve your credit and increase your score. Some important things to know before adding authorized users to your account.

- **Note: Be sure you know what the balance is or make sure that its under 30% of the credit card limit. No use in adding an authorized user to your file if it's over 50% or maxed out.**

Before adding Citi, Capital One, Discover authorized users please note these credit card companies now require that you send in ID and SSN copies. So, if you have a CPN file, they won't be added if you didn't set up a proper foundation with your CPN like public Directories.

If you are adding an Authorized User to get higher funding, add 1 to 2 AUs (authorized users) that are at least 2 years old and minimum of $8000 credit limit. Anything less won't make that much of an impact. The bigger the limit, the better!

- **Recommended AU Provider: BusinessFinancialSuite.com**

PRIMARY TRADELINES

Primary tradelines have always meant one thing: an account on a credit report for which the primary account holder is listed as the primary account holder.

This is in contrast to piggybacking off of Authorized User tradeline, where the account history reports on the authorized user's credit report (as an authorized user… not a primary account holder).

- **Recommended CPN Friendly Primary Tradeline Credit Cards: firstprogress.com, deserve.com, zblackcard.com or openskycc.com**
- **Recommended Primary Tradelines: horizoncardservices.com, fingerhut.com, selflender.com, myjewelersclub.com, huttonchase.com, newcoastdirect.com and rentreporters.com**

chapter 6

Business Classification Codes

STANDARD INDUSTRIAL CLASSIFICATION (SIC)

Selecting the right business classification codes are extremely important. Avoid selecting codes that will trigger a red flag with the business credit bureaus and lenders. This can stop your business credit building efforts dead in its tracks.

The **Standard Industrial Classification** (SIC) is a system for classifying industries by a four-digit code. Established in the United States in 1937, it is used by government agencies to classify industry areas.

The SIC codes can be grouped into progressively broader industry classifications:

- **industry group, major group and division.**

The first 3 digits of the SIC code indicate the industry group, and the first two digits indicate the major group. Each division encompasses a range of SIC codes

Some small business SIC Codes can trigger automatic turndowns, higher premiums and reduced credit limit recommendations on your business credit files.

- Note: SIC and NAICS Codes -- while the codes you choose for your business are entirely up to you, I encourage all of my clients NOT to use codes for investments of any kind as these are HIGH RISK codes.

- Recommended codes for investment business: SIC Code 8741-98 Management Services and NAICS Code 541611 General Management Consulting Services or Business Management Services.

Visit this link to see which SIC code refers to your corporation: https://www.osha.gov/pls/imis/sic_manual.html

If you chose to use another code besides the one provided above, please refer to the link above and search for the code you desire. This is a decision you must make for the entity.

NORTH AMERICAN INDUSTRY CLASSIFICATION SYSTEM (NAICS)

You will also need a NAICS Code. This is the **North American Industry Classification System (NAICS)**.

In the United States the SIC code is being supplanted by the six-digit **North American Industry Classification System** (NAICS code), which was released in 1997; however certain government departments and agencies, such as the U.S. Securities and Exchange Commission (SEC), still use the SIC codes.

Visit this link to see which NAICS code refers to your corporation: https://www.census.gov/eos/www/naics

- **HIGH RISK CODES: Construction / Real Estate Investing / Investments / Car Sales / Adult Entertainment / Travel Industry / Money Lending / Collecting / Restaurants & Dry Cleaners**

You still will be able to perform the above businesses, but you will have to create a separate division under the corporation. This division will perform the real estate investing, construction, the investments, marketing & advertising, training and development etc.

As you can see selecting the wrong business SIC and NAICS codes can get your business labeled as a high risk and directly impact your financing ability, insurance premiums, and credit limit recommendations.

Please don't make this small mistake that can cost your business future problems.

CHAPTER 7

Business Credit Profile Setup

DUN & BRADSTREET

Dun & Bradstreet is a corporation that offers information on commercial credit as well as reports on businesses. Most notably, Dun & Bradstreet is recognizable for its Data Universal Numbering System (DUNS numbers); these generate business information reports for more than 100 million companies around the globe.

Visit link to Apply for your Duns Number:
https://www.dnb.com/duns-number/get-a-duns.html

Search to see if your entity is in their database already. If so, select your entity and proceed with updating your file. Set up a complete profile with Dun and Bradstreet – Simply obtaining a DUNs number doesn't cut it. You will need to furnish additional information on your profile to give creditors a complete picture of your business.

Add existing positive trade references – if you have existing trade references to add to your file then you may want to consider using DNB's business credit builder program which allows you to add your own references but keep in mind there are certain references they will not accept.

Please be advised: there is a fee for this service. If you use the vendors noted in this blueprint, you will not have to pay to add anything. The vendors will automatically report your activity, when you place orders and make payments.

- **Note: D&B will email you your ID# in 30 days. When you receive your ID#, go to iupdate.com, create username and password. Your email notification will provide all the details. Once you have your ID# you can go back in and provide complete company information.**

**Be prepared! Dun and Bradstreet will call to verify the information you provided. Do Not check your file every day! This will RED FLAG your file. Check you file once every 2-3 months on a Sunday evening.

You want to provide complete details for the following sections:

Company Name: Enter Corporation Name
Physical Address: Enter address or virtual office (No PO Boxes)
Physical City: Enter city
Physical Zip: Enter zip
Telephone: Enter phone #
Chief Executive: Enter your name or partner name
Year Started: Enter Year
Employees: 5-6
SIC: 8741
Line of Business: Management Services
List your officers: NAME, CFO NAME, VICE PRESIDENT NAME, CHIEF ENGINEER NAME, GENERAL MANAGER
Banking & Finance Section: If you have financials enter them. If not, you can add them later.

You may have to contact D&B for assistance when it comes to uploading files. Be prepared to pay their fees! This is optional

and not needed unless you just want to provide the documents.

EXPERIAN BUSINESS

A small business credit score is vital for separating your personal and business financial risk. As a forward-thinking small business owner, you know that credit affects your ability to obtain capital to develop your small business.

- **Your business credit report can influence: The amount of your loan and what interest rates you'll pay, your business insurance premiums and Whether suppliers will extend credit terms.**

Experian's small business credit reports can help you establish, improve and monitor your business credit score. So, you get the funding and credit you need, when you need it.

Set up a complete profile with Experian Business. You will provide the same information as you provided to Dun and Bradstreet.

- **Visit link to Apply for your Experian Business Profile: https://sbcr.experian.com/pdp.aspx?pg=sample&hdr=pp&link=5502&offercode=sbcredit**

EQUIFAX COMMERCIAL

Equifax is the last on this list of the main credit bureaus for business. Once you have these lines in place, and you make your payments on time, your small business credit will begin to take shape.

With Equifax, they provide small businesses credit services to help the business keep its credit on track and improve credit scores. Getting a business registered with Equifax takes only a few minutes but is worth the time because it results in being able to use the services Equifax provides businesses.

You have to buy a product or service from Equifax. According to the Equifax FAQs page, any business that wants to register their business must first purchase a product or service. This will automatically take the business owner or representative to the registration process. Complete the registration information. The six-step registration process requires first buying a product, which is the first two steps of the process, then completing the ePort registration information.

The ePort registration information will require the account number and security numbers given with the purchase to identify the company, agreement of the company policies and business contact information. A confirmation email is sent upon completion of the information.

- **Note: Make sure all information about your business matches the details you choose from (page 3– Corporation Image) before submitting your application to Equifax.**

Sign into the ePort section of the Equifax website. Use the account number and security numbers given previously to sign into Equifax. This completes the registration of a business with Equifax.

Establishing credit with companies that report to this credit bureau will help you start trade lines through Equifax for business. Trade lines can help you build your small business credit so that your company can qualify for loans and bigger lines of credit in the future.

Set up a complete profile with Equifax Business. You will provide the same information as you provided to Dun and Bradstreet and Experian Business.

- **Visit link to Apply for your Experian Business Profile: https://www.equifax.com/business/business-credit-reports-small-business/**

TAX FILING

March 17, xxxx (estimated tax date for corporations)

- **Check with IRS for deadlines: https://www.irs.gov/businesses/small-businesses-self-employed/filing-and-paying-your-business-taxes**

Corporate tax returns (Forms 1120, 1120A, and 1120S) for the year 20XX, or to request automatic 6-month extension of time to file (Form 7004) for corporations who use the calendar year as their tax year.

**(The normal deadline for corporate returns is March 15th, but this falls on a Saturday, so the deadline is pushed to the next business day, which is Monday, March 17th.)

You must file with or without business activity. Form FTB 100 is filed when you hire personnel.

Your goal within the first 12 months of business is to get to the profit zone. Create a business that will offset the tax fee and continue to move forward with developing your business.

**Please note: You will file taxes for the entity: C CORP, S CORP, LLC, NONPROFIT--- according to the rules and regulations of "your state" in which the business is located.

Chapter 8

Revolving Credit Cards

You only need to start with 3 revolving accounts. You will need to provide your SSN for these accounts, if you have bad personal credit follow instructions on pages 19-21 and fix your credit with Authorized Users and Primary Tradelines or if you used an CPN, make sure your credit score is above 700 and strong.

Process your revolving accounts like you processed your vendor accounts. Charge up to 20% on the line and then pay it back on time.

- **Recommended Credit Cards: Bank of America, Wells Fargo, American Express, Capital One, Chase Bank, Citibank and US Bank**

Please note the four tiers of credit. Amounts will vary according to credit files and personal credit scores. Please be ready to guarantee each account. Please be mindful of annual fees and rates.

Tier One Creditors:
Net-30 Accounts (3-4) with average credit limits $500- $1,500.

Tier Two Creditors:
Low-end Revolving Accounts (3-4) with average credit limits $1500- $2500.

Tier Three Creditors:
Mid-range Revolving Accounts (3-4) with average credit limits
$2500 - $7000.
Tier Four Creditors:
High-end Revolving Accounts (2-4) with average credit limits
$40,000--$50,000.

This tier will include your MasterCard, VISA, Discover, and American Express business accounts. These lines report on your business credit files. Not your personal credit files.

As you go through this process and your accounts start to report you will begin to get offers in the mail. Keep and organize those offers. This will make getting more credit easy for you. Remember to pay invoices on time. Set a time limit for yourself. Select a goal and push it into the market creating an income for the corporation/entity.

Revenue in the corporate bank account gives you access to business lines of credit and moves the corporation up the 3-tier levels of credit qualifying it for bank level financing.

* Don't get caught up in the hype thinking you need 100 plus credit cards. Start with 3 vendors / 3 credit cards and this will put the corporation on the right path. Make sure you review the details of cash advances on corporate cards. Every 3-6 months complete more applications until you reach your desired amount of funding. Complete up to 3 applications at one time.

HOW TO FILL OUT APPLICATIONS TO GET APPROVED

Complete the below with the information on the corporation.

ABOUT YOUR BUSINESS SECTION:

Legal name of business: Business Street Address (no PO BOXES)
City, State, Zip Code
Business Email Address:
Business Phone Number
EIN #
Annual Business Revenue / Sales $250,000 - do not go over this
amount – use this projected amount if a new corporation/entity.
If you have financials use that amount.
Nature of Business: (stay away from high risk category - visit page
23)
Number of Employees: 5
Type of Business: Corporation / or list entity type
How Long in Business? 2-5 years (doesn't matter if true or not)
**if less than 1 year – use a division start date. Division must be
set up in order to use that date. This gives new corporation/entity
aging or seasoning.

Take the time to study your credit applications. Go online and look
at what lenders ask for.

ABOUT YOURSELF or PARTNER SECTION:

Your Name:
Your Address: Enter business address City, State, Zip Code
Home Phone #
DOB
Social Security Number: Use your SS# or partner SS# Or CPN

**(Make sure you cross out the word SSN & write CPN
instead)**

Gross Annual: $147,000 – use this projected amount for new corporation. Established corporations use your financials.

Job Title as Authorizing Officer: President / CFO

EMPLOYEE CARDS Leave this section blank for now - after you get approved ask for employee cards.

TRANSFER BALANCES: Leave blank Sign application.

Call the number on the credit application to get status reports on the approval decision. Please keep all reference #'s provided.

HOW TO INCREASE AMOUNTS ON CREDIT CARDS

1. Before activating the card, before using the card --- call and ask for an increase amount. If they say no - ask for a rate decrease. Sometimes the answer is a yes and sometimes a no.

2. After 6 months of using the card and on-time payments. Call or write and ask for an increase or rate decrease.

3. Make sure you are aware of additional fees the card may carry, such as annual fees, late fees, etc. Some cards, such as AMEX (Gold or Platinum) carry an annual fee of $450 with the first year waived.

Chapter 9

Bank Loans

Everyone starts somewhere. The process of building a business credit profile isn't incredibly different from building personal credit; making payments on time and avoiding carrying high balances are always good practices, but the tools will be different. Many business owners will start out with credit cards specifically designed for startups or those with little to no business credit history, but after time, you'll likely be looking to graduate to bigger products that can help your business grow and allow you to expand your credit profile.

Here, then, are 5 business loans that can help build your business credit.

1. **Chase Business Term Loans**
   Most banks will offer business loans or other basic business financing options, but Chase can boast your report to all major commercial credit agencies (Dun & Bradstreet, Equifax, Experian, SBFE). That means that as you make your payments on time and keep your balance down with a Chase loan, your diligence and hard work will likely reflect on your business credit report, more likely than with most other major lenders.

   Chase business term loans start at $5,000, offer fixed and adjustable rates, and fixed monthly payments to help you keep a grip on your cash flow. They also offer lines of credit, commercial mortgages, equipment financing, and, of course, credit cards.

2. **Citi Business Loans**
   Similar to Chase, Citi reports to all major business credit bureaus. They also offer a wide variety of credit products from term loans to lines of credit to commercial mortgages. With their reporting procedures, you can add positive history to your business credit profile.

   They also offer a service online that prompts you to fill out a worksheet regarding your business needs to be contacted by a Citi lender to discuss further.

3. **SBA Microloans**
   Most lenders require that your business have at least two years in operation before approving you for financing. The Small Business Association, along with offering some of the savory products for veteran small businesses also offer microloans for younger businesses.

   Microloans cap out at $50,000, and the average amount is around $13,000. It's a great option for those starting a business or continuing to get their fledgling operation off the ground, and a solid way to build a business credit history.

4. **Microloan by Kiva**
   A non-profit lender designed to help struggling entrepreneurs, Kiva offers 0% APR loans of up to $10,000, all funds coming from a strong community brought together by a desire to help small businesses flourish.

   As if 0% interest isn't enough of a reason to check it out, they also promise to report your good payments to the business credit bureaus, giving your business credit profile some positive marks.

Accion Microloans

Another microlender, Accion seeks to help business owners with less-than-excellent credit or who have been in business for just a few months. They require a minimum personal credit score of 575 and lend up to $10,000. Like Kiva, Accion is funded by investors and the donations of a community of people who care about small businesses and a strong economy.

If your business credit isn't awesome or just needs a few more miles on it, there are certainly options for you. Again, the best practices you've learned all your life about personal credit, basic things like paying early or on time, and carrying low balances, can help keep your score healthy and contribute to a strong and sustainable business.

HOW TO GET A BANK LOAN

Step 1 - take two revolving credit cards and pull $5,000 off each. Be mindful of cash advance fees!

Step 2 - place money $10,000 in corporate bank account to sit for 3 months

Step 3 - tell the bank associate you want to apply for a loan secured against your $10,000 checking account.

Step 4- if bank won't allow steps 1-3 apply for a CD and borrow against it

Step 5 - use funds to pay back credit cards in step 1

Please note: this is an optional strategy, which can be used depending upon the goals of the corporation/entity. Please be aware of all rates, fees and restrictions before moving forward.

Chapter 10

Government Contracts and Grants

GOVERNMENT CONTRACTS

Now that you have learned the steps it takes to build your business credit and accessing funding for your business. Let's take it another step further in your quest to achieving financial success in government contracts.

The United States government buys lots of products and services from US businesses. With the approximately $500 billion in government contracts it awards each year, nearly a quarter are legally required to go to small businesses that have navigated the process of how to get government contracts.

- **Note: Contract Spending Data at https://datalab.usaspending.gov/contract-explorer.html**

What exactly are these highly desired opportunities for your small business, and how can you cash in?

It's a good question—although not the simplest answer. Above all else, government contracting is an extremely competitive field, especially for small businesses but you will learn how to obtain them in this 30 Days 50k book.

Even though federal law requires the government to provide opportunities for small businesses, a huge number of small businesses all bid to get the same contracts.
It's not surprising—after all, don't you want one?
41

Doesn't everyone? They're big jobs, which means big money.

All of that competition can pose difficulties for new companies looking into how to get government contracts. But once you're registered and in the government's databases, it can be a lot easier to get government contracts for small business.

Since there's a lot that goes into the process of how to get government contracts for small business, I will break it down step by step. By the end, you'll know how to register your small business to apply for contracts. And all the effort will be worth it once you've been awarded your first government contract.

TYPES OF GOVERNMENT CONTRACTORS

Prime Contractors

In order to get government contracts, you'll have to decide what kind of contractor you'll be. There are two types of government contractors: Prime Contractors and Subcontractors.

Prime contractors are those that bid for and subsequently win contracts directly from government agencies. Subcontractors join prime contractors' teams and provide a specific capability or product that the prime contractor requires. These contractors generally have a more honed area of expertise.

Prime contractors are legally responsible for all aspects of a government contract. Since they're fulfilling all of the work, this means that they have to oversee this contract the way they would a small business—such as hiring other employees (like subcontractors, for instance) and ensuring the government contract is carried out until complete.

Prime contractors include lots of industries, with businesses focused on fields as different as animal control services and law research.

- **examples of businesses that commonly operate as prime contractors: construction companies, scientific research labs, IT support services, and service-based companies in industries such as transportation and disposal.**

Contracts for prime contractors are more competitive than those for subcontractors, and there is definitely more work and risk involved. But with that scope does come more control and a bigger payoff.

Subcontractors

Subcontractors enjoy the luxury of not having full responsibility for the entire contract but rather for a small area of specialization.

This is a great way to get involved in government contracting as you can build valuable experience (called "past performance") that will help you qualify for future contracts. Think of it like building your business's credit!

Starting as a subcontractor can be a great way to get your legs in government contracting, and you'll probably make more contacts if you tagalong with a well-established prime contractor.

REGISTER YOUR BUSINESS TO GET GOVERNMENT CONTRACTS

System for Award Management (SAM)

The federal government's System for Award Management (SAM) will be your main point of contact for your contracts, and it's also where you'll register to get contracts for the first time too.

- **Note: Register your business at SAM here https://www.sam.gov/portal/SAM/##11#1**

As a small business, you'll create a user account, register your business with the US government for free (or update or renew an existing registration if you've inherited a business that may have competed for government contracts before). You can expect an average of 7-10 days for your registration to process, during which SAM will request validation of your business from outside parties such as the IRS.

SAM also works as a database for government agencies and contractors to seek subcontractors to fulfill their contracts, so it's important to keep your registration up-to-date. After your registration is approved, you will automatically be input into the SBA's database, the Dynamic Small Business Search (DSBS), a database similar to SAM.

- **Note: DSBS database here http://dsbs.sba.gov/dsbs/search/dsp_dsbs.cfm**

Government agencies and contractor offices will use both of these databases to fill their contracting needs. But a huge part of how to get government contracts is bidding for contracts on your own—so you'll be using this system a lot.

Once you've registered your business in SAM and confirmed your approval, it's time to finally find out exactly how to get government contracts. At this point, you'll need to have made your decision as to whether you're going to be a prime contractor or a subcontractor

- **Note: Prime Contractors are responsible for the full deal, whereas Subcontractors join contracts to fill a specific task.**

FIND GOVERNMENT CONTRACT OPPORTUNITIES

1. **System for Award Management (SAM):** The same site your business uses to apply for government contracts is the same site government agencies use to locate available contractors, System for Award Management (SAM). Because businesses search the SAM database by many different factors including capabilities, size, location, experience, and ownership, it's invaluable, so be sure to fill out your business profile thoroughly.
   **(Go to page 44 for details)

2. **Dynamic Small Business Search (DSBS):** The SBA's own database also serves as a database for contracting offices to search for small business contractors.
   The Dynamic Small Business Search (DSBS) is also where prime contractors will search for subcontractors or other small business to team up with on a joint venture contract. Again, make sure your SAM business profile is completely filled out since that information automatically carries over to the DSBS database.
   **(Go to page 44 for details.)

3. **FedBizOpps:** Opportunities for contractors are also listed at FedBizOpps, a site that federal agencies are required to use to post available contracts that are valued at more than $25,000. Think about it as a job board for contractors.
   - **visit FedBizOpps here: https://www.fbo.gov**

4. **GSA Schedules Program:** To connect with a government contract opportunity to provide millions of products for volume discount prices, look on the GSA Schedules Program. You'll need to go through another round of registration in order to join the program, but it can be worth it for these kinds of contracts.
   - **visit GSA here: https://www.gsa.gov/buying-selling/purchasing-programs/gsa-schedules**

5. **SUB-Net:** If you're a prime contractor looking to fill subcontractor spots (or a subcontractor hoping to score one), SUB-Net is a great place to start. As part of their government contract, prime contractors are required to provide subcontracting opportunities. SUB-Net is where those subcontracting opportunities are listed. Once your business is registered with the government, you can apply for these opportunities.
   - **visit SUB-Net here: https://eweb.sba.gov/gls/dsp_sbabanner.cfm**

6. **USASpending:** You can also visit USASpending, which lists each contract the federal government awards, plus accompanying details. You'll be able to view the amount of the award, funding agency, and the unique identifier of the business that received the award. This is also an easy way to track the government's purchasing habits and potential opportunities.
   - **visit USASpending here: https://www.usaspending.gov/#/**

7. **Office of Small and Disadvantaged Business Utilization (OSDBU):** Many of the federal agencies that purchase from small businesses also have an office dedicated to identifying opportunities that small businesses can fulfill. These offices can be called the Office of Small and Disadvantaged Business Utilization or Office of Small Business Programs, and their involvement differs depending on the agency they service. It's a good idea to reach out to the OSDBU of the contract's agency when you've found a contract that may work for you.
   visit OSDBU here:
   https://www.dol.gov/oasam/programs/osdbu/sbrefa/

8. **Capalino + Company:** Small businesses just getting into government contracting can also reach out to consulting companies like Capalino + Company. These companies work with small businesses to develop strategies around a business's strengths and a government agency's needs to secure government contracts. Although Capalino specifically works within the New York State area, there are plenty of different companies that specialize in regions across the country to assist both for-profit and not-for-profit entities with contracts.
   - **visit Capalino here:**
   https://www.capalino.com/services/securing-government-contracts/

How to Get Government Contracts

There are seven essential steps in getting a government contract for your small business. Each involves a lot more breakdown on its own. But here's the important process to follow to make sure you're both qualified to receive government contracts and registered in the government's database to do business:

1. Read about the different types of government contracts available to small businesses.
   - **Note: Types of government contracts https://www.sba.gov/federal-contracting**

2. Calculate your business's most recent total annual revenue.

3. Find your business's North American Industry Classification System (NAICS) code with the US Census index. **(Go back to page 32 for NAICS details.)**

4. Check whether your business qualifies for government contracting opportunities on the SBA's prequalification quiz.
   - **Note: SBA Prequalification Quiz at https://www.sba.gov/size-standards**

5. Register your business on System for Award Management (SAM) using the NAICS code and your total annual revenue on the SAM database.
   - **Note: Register your business at SAM at https://www.sam.gov/portal/SAM/##11#1**

6. Decide whether your business will seek contracts as a subcontractor or a prime contractor.
7. Begin bidding for government contracts by searching through FedBizOpps, the GSA Schedules Program, SUB-Net, USASpending.Gov, and OSDBU.Gov, depending on your type of business.

Once You Know How to Get Government Contracts, You'll Be Off to the Races.

Government contracting for your small business and leaping into the field is a big undertaking. But taking steps and learning how to get government contracts will pay off sooner rather than later—your business will quickly gain experience for any other opportunities that come your way.

Since the field for government contracts is highly competitive—and getting more competitive each day—you might not score a contract right away. But your small business will find its niche. And since the field is growing, more opportunities are popping up all the time—especially if you begin as a subcontractor.

- **Note: Be sure to note trends and patterns with how government agencies are spending money. Keep track of which small businesses are receiving money and what their industries are, plus what contracts are being awarded and when.**

Staying ahead of trends can help inform your betting to find out which government contracts your business is most likely to win. Contractors can also keep an eye out for federal contract trending forecasts that explore the upcoming fiscal year's trends—to make sure you get in on the action.

- **Visit Government Contracts Forecast here:
  https://hallways.cap.gsa.gov/app/#/x/forecast-of-
  contracting-opportunities**

GOVERNMENT GRANTS

"Free money." If you're starting a business or running a business, nothing sounds better. Unlike business loans, you don't have to repay small business grants, so there's no worry over term length, interest rates, APR, refinancing or business credit. You just need to apply, qualify, and boom—free money.

There are two caveats, though. First, small business grants are generally specific about what you can spend the money on, whereas small business loans tend to be very flexible.

For example, if you score a grant for developing a new kind of environmentally-friendly lemonade stand, then you'll likely have to spend the money on equipment or research, not on buying lemons and sugar.

Second, and maybe most importantly, small business grants are hard to qualify for—and even harder to find. There's a lot of misinformation, dead old websites, confusing databases, complicated government restrictions, discontinued contests, and more out there. With this book you don't have to worry about all that.

Thanks to 30 Days 50K book, I have compiled a list of verified startup grants and small business grants for you to check out while your building your business credit.

SMALL BUSINESS GRANTS: FEDERAL

Although there are plenty of federal small business grants, they are primarily open to companies in the science, technology, or health fields.

If your business is involved in research and development or in scientific initiatives—including environmental and climate initiatives—then federal grant programs might be able to cover some of your expenses.

Sometimes, grant winners receive the funding directly from the federal government. However, in most cases, the federal government just determines eligibility but doles out grant money to state and local governments. States and localities then distribute the funds to small businesses.

1. **Small Business Innovation Research Program**
   The SBIR encourages small businesses engaged in research and development that has commercial potential. The SBIR aims to stimulate technological innovation and scientific entrepreneurship. Eleven government agencies participate in the program, and each creates their own eligibility guidelines, research and development topics, and reviews applications. Grants start at $150,000, but if your business shows promise, then you can receive additional grants of up to $1 million.

   - **Visit HERE: https://www.sbir.gov/about/about-sbir**

2. **Small Business Technology Transfer Program**
the STTR has similar goals but requires its small
business applicants to collaborate with a research
institution. Five federal agencies currently participate in
in this program, setting aside a bit of their budget to
work with small businesses. As with the SBIR grants,
these grants start at $150,000 and then go up to $1
million. That's where this small business grant comes
into play. Let's take a quick look at the five main federal
agencies that participate in the SBIR and STTR
programs.
   * **Visit HERE: https://www.sbir.gov/about/about-sttr**

3. **National Science Foundation**
The NSF accepts proposals in the areas of engineering,
science, or medicine, though specific topics change from
year to year. They even have a YouTube channel to help
you get your application in order.
   * **Visit HERE: https://seedfund.nsf.gov/**

4. **NASA**
What's cooler than collaborating with NASA?
Getting *paid* to collaborate with NASA. Plenty of
technology sectors are important to develop for NASA,
but they're especially interested in energy efficiency or
alternative and renewable energy or efficient ways of
building spacecrafts. 3, 2, 1, lift-off.
   * **Visit HERE:**
     https://sbir.gsfc.nasa.gov/content/nasa-sbirsttr-basics

5. **National Institutes of Health**
   The National Institutes of Health, a subset of the Department of Health & Human Services, offers small business grants to companies researching and developing commercially innovative biomedical technologies. Sound like you? Save some money while you're saving lives.
   - **Visit HERE: https://sbir.nih.gov/**

6. **Department of Energy**
   The Energy Department's Office of Science also participates in these two small business grants. Topics include environmental science, clean energy, and material science. Check out their hour-long program overview webinar for more details.
   - **Visit HERE: https://science.energy.gov/sbir/**

7. **Department of Defense**
   Whether your technology research and development are meant for the Army, Navy, Air Force, or DARPA's advanced initiatives, the Department of Defense will help you fund and commercialize your products. There are also a few governmental agencies that offer small business grants for the Small Business Innovation Research program only. The STTR mandates collaboration between a research institution and your small business, but the SBIR does not—which could be an advantage or a disadvantage, depending on what you're looking for.
   - **Visit HERE: https://sbir.defensebusiness.org/?AspxAutoDetectCoo kieSupport=1**

8. **National Institute of Food & Agriculture**
   This branch of the Department of Agriculture supports research and development in the agricultural field specifically. Topics include forestry, food science and nutrition, aqua cultural, biofuel products, animal protection, and more.
   - **Visit HERE: https://nifa.usda.gov/program/small-business-innovation-research-program-sbir**

9. **National Institute of Standards & Technology**
   A division of the Department of Commerce, NIST gives small business grants to companies developing technology under topics like cybersecurity, manufacturing, software, and trade. Note that it also deals with energy, healthcare, and others—you're free to apply to some or all of these departments if you qualify for the SBIR!
   - **Visit HERE: https://www.nist.gov/about-nist/funding-opportunities**

10. **Environmental Protection Agency**
    The EPA rewards businesses looking to advance green technology and sustainable scientific developments.
    - **Visit HERE: https://www.epa.gov/sbir**

11. **Department of Transportation**
    The Department of Transportation's transportation systems center, Volpe, accepts solicitations for aid in developing technology regarding aviation, railroads, and highways, but make sure to check their updated topic listings before you apply.
    - **Visit HERE: https://www.volpe.dot.gov/work-with-us/small-business-innovation-research**

12. **Homeland Security**
    The Department of Homeland Security provides grants
    to small businesses that work in the areas of border and
    maritime security, chemical and biological defense,
    cyber security, explosives, or first responder group
    technology.
    - **Visit HERE: https://sbir2.st.dhs.gov/portal/SBIR/**

13. **Department of Education**
    The Department of Education's SBIR grant topics are
    listed under the National Center for Education
    Research branch and range from pre-reading and pre-
    writing technology developments to research that deals
    with STEM skills, language learning, and behavioral
    learning patterns.
    - **Visit HERE:
      https://www2.ed.gov/programs/sbir/index.html**

14. **National Oceanic & Atmospheric Administration**
    The Technology Partnerships Office of NOAA offers
    small business grants for developments and research in
    coastline communities and economies, healthy ocean
    monitoring, climate adaptation and mitigation, and much
    more. I trawled through a few databases of Federal small
    business grants--of which the Catalog of Federal
    Domestic Assistance is the authoritative source--and
    pulled the most important. Still, make sure to search
    yourself, especially if your small business is involved in
    agriculture, public health, or sustainable development!
    These offerings update regularly.
    - **Visit HERE: https://techpartnerships.noaa.gov/SBIR**

15. **Rural Energy for America Program**
    This grant program, run by the Department of
    Agriculture, centers on small businesses in eligible rural
    areas looking to purchase, construct, or install renewable
    energy systems or energy efficiency improvement
    technologies. You can partner it with a USDA loan
    guaranty as well, and together they'll back up to 75% of
    your eligible project costs.
    - **Visit HERE: https://www.rd.usda.gov/programs-services/rural-energy-america-program-renewable-energy-systems-energy-efficiency**

16. **Value Added Producer Grant**
    If you're an agricultural producer, the VAPG
    program could help with you with working capital
    expenses, ranging from processing, to marketing and
    advertising, to inventory and salary expenses.
    - **Visit HERE: https://www.rd.usda.gov/programs-services/value-added-producer-grants**

17. **Distance Learning and Telemedicine Grant**
    The Department of Agriculture offers this grant
    program for small businesses and agricultural producers
    that are modernizing education and health in rural
    communities. Specifically, these grants are an option if
    your company provides education or health services
    through telecommunications. Awards range from
    $50,000 to $500,000.
    - **Visit HERE: https://www.rd.usda.gov/programs-services/distance-learning-telemedicine-grants**

18. **3D Elevation Grant**
    The Department of the Interior is offering a grant to small businesses that can creatively leverage lidar and map data to come up with natural 3D imaging of the nation's topographical boundaries. This is a great grant for design and technology firms.
    - **Visit HERE: https://www.usgs.gov/core-science-systems/ngp/3dep/what-is-3dep**

19. **CyberTipline Grant**
    This grant program, run by the Department of Homeland Security, offers money to small businesses that provide services and programs that help prevent sex trafficking and exploitation of children.
    - **Visit HERE: https://www.grantsolutions.gov/gs/preaward/preview PublicAnnouncement.do?id=62685**

SMALL BUSINESS GRANTS: STATE

State-level small business grants are generally geared towards that particular state's social or economic concerns. That said, they're much more accessible due to lower competition. Also, many are matching grants: instead of just providing the funds for you to use for a certain purpose, some will require that you match the money they give as well.

- **Note: You can search for grants your own state and industry by looking at your state's department of commerce website or grants portal. Also, while I list these state-specific small business grants, many of these runs across multiple states, so don't give up if the grant looks right but your states don't match!**

1. **Arizona Commerce Authority**
   The Arizona Commerce Authority is a great resource for small business owners in AZ. Check back throughout the year for new competitions and grant options. The Arizona Step Grant is a popular program, which offers money to small businesses that are exporting products or expanding into international markets.
   - **Visit HERE: https://www.azcommerce.com/**

2. **Arkansas Technology Transfer Assistance Grant Program**
   The Arkansas Economic Development Commission offers several grants, rebates, and incentives to businesses that create jobs or expand in Arkansas. For example, the Infrastructure Grant is for businesses that create full-time jobs in Arkansas.
   - **Visit HERE: https://www.arkansasedc.com/why-arkansas/business-climate/incentives/pages/job-creation-incentives**

3. **Colorado Export Development Grant**
   Colorado regularly ranks as one of the best states for startups and entrepreneurship, and the state government is helping to make sure that innovation continues in this state. Colorado offers grants for many types of small and medium sized businesses, especially businesses that are interested in international development or that are involved in advanced industries like robotics.
   - **Visit HERE: https://choosecolorado.com/doing-business/incentives-financing/startups-small-business/**

4. **DC Small and Local Business Grant**
   The DC Department of Small and Local Business has multiple open grant opportunities for businesses in particular "wards" of the city. You can keep track of the ongoing grant opportunities on their Current Solicitations & Opportunities site. They tend to offer the most grants to retail businesses that are revitalizing downtown neighborhoods.
   - **Visit HERE: https://dslbd.dc.gov/service/current-solicitations-opportunities**

5. **Idaho State Trade Expansion Program (STEP) Grant**
   Many states actually have a STEP program, Idaho included. However, they each have individual application processes and qualification criteria, so make sure you double-check what you need to do to apply! In Idaho, these grants are primarily for businesses that want to enter international markets.
   - **Visit HERE: https://commerce.idaho.gov/idaho-business/international-trade/step-grant/**

6. **Illinois Recycling Expansion and Modernization Program**
   Sustainability-driven small businesses in Illinois (and other states) should consider the REM program, which offers grants of up to $250,000. Note that this is a matching grant program, so you'll have to put up your own cash to receive the government's—budget well in advance if you're aiming for this opportunity.
   - **Visit HERE: https://www.iira.org/rdrg/recycling-expansion-and-modernization-rem-program/**

7. **Iowa Business Development Grant**
   Recycling Iowa provides a wide range of business development grants. The state's focus is on businesses that create manufacturing jobs and enhance Iowa's other industries. There are also grants for retail businesses which are rehabilitating downtown buildings. You can see the latest opportunities on Iowa's grants portal.
   - **Visit HERE:**
     https://www.iowagrants.gov/outsideStorefrontList.jsp?type=Grant

8. **Kansas Job Creation Fund**
   Kansas's Job Creation Fund gives grants to businesses looking for help establishing themselves in Kansas. The fund typically disburses the grant money to recipients over three years as their company reaches certain investment and employment benchmarks.
   - **Visit HERE:**
     http://kanview.ks.gov/EcoDev/ProgramDetails.aspx?id=JCF

9. **Louisiana Community Development Block Grant**
   The Office of Community Development aims to improve the living environments and economic opportunities for Louisiana's low-income residents. While small businesses can't apply directly, contact the state or local government branches most relevant to your business's function and see if you can receive that funding to do community work. There are also disaster recovery grants to businesses that are were affected by hurricanes.
   - **Visit HERE:**
     https://www.doa.la.gov/Pages/ocd/Index.aspx

10. **Maryland Child Care Quality Incentive Grant Program**
The Maryland Division of Early Childhood Development recently reopened its CCQIG program for local childcare facilities. The grant is awarded quarterly.
- **Visit HERE:**
https://earlychildhood.marylandpublicschools.org/child-care-providers/credentialing/child-care-quality-incentive-grant-program

11. **ExportMD Program**
For those especially enterprising small businesses: if you're looking to market internationally, then this program could help you cut down on costs.
- **Visit HERE:**
http://commerce.maryland.gov/fund/programs-for-businesses/exportmd-program

12. **Maryland Economic Development Assistance Authority & Fund**
Although we happen to be listing a lot of Maryland initiatives, many states carry the same or similar programs in their own boundaries as well. In this case, the MEDAAF is an unusually broad small business grant and loan opportunity for Maryland small business owners, so don't miss it. Priority funding areas and industries vary with each grant cycle, so keep an eye out for updates.
- **Visit HERE:**
http://commerce.maryland.gov/fund/programs-for-businesses/medaaf

13. **Minnesota Dairy Business Planning Grant**
    On the other side of the spectrum, this program covers a narrow sliver of Minnesota's small businesses—but that means low competition. If you manage a dairy farm or are developing environmental technologies related to dairy farming, look into the DBPG.
    - **Visit HERE:**
      http://www.mda.state.mn.us/funding?field_category_target_id=5

14. **Minnesota REETAIN**
    REETAIN, or Retaining Early Educators Through Attaining Incentives Now, offers small grants to child care professionals in Minnesota. If you're a child care professional in Minnesota, this could be that extra cash you need to help defray costs.
    - **Visit HERE:**
      http://www.childcareawaremn.org/providers/grants-and-scholarships/reetain-bonuses/

15. **Minnesota Crop Research Grant Program**
    Again, most state's agriculture departments have small business grants that are some variation on the CRGP. If your business researches agricultural product quality, quantity, or value, this grant could work well for you.
    - **Visit HERE:**
      http://www.mda.state.mn.us/funding?field_category_target_id=5

16. **Minnesota Innovation Voucher Award Program**
    If your business needs cash to purchase technical
    assistance or to commercialize your products, you
    can score a substantial amount of capital with this grant.
    This is a matching grant, so you'll need to put up half of
    the cash.
    - **Visit HERE:**
      **https://mn.gov/deed/business/financing-
      business/deed-programs/mn-jcf/**

17. **Minnesota Job Creation Fund**
    The Minnesota Job Creation Fund is for new and
    expanding businesses that meet targets for job creation
    and capital investment. Eligible companies can receive
    up to $1 million for creating or retaining high-salaried
    jobs and for rehabilitating facilities.
    - **Visit HERE:**
      **https://mn.gov/deed/business/financing-
      business/deed-programs/mn-jcf/**

18. **Nebraska Child Care Grant**
    For child care homes and centers, this program offers a
    number of smaller grants for you to apply to.
    - **Visit HERE:**
      **http://dhhs.ne.gov/children_family_services/ChildCar
      e/Pages/Grants.aspx**

19. **New York City Commute Enhancement Grant**
    Up to $10,000, the NYCCE grant can apply to a number
    of initiatives related to city commuting. If you're a New
    York small business with a toe in transportation,
    applying here is a must.
    - **Visit HERE: (Continue on NEXT page)**

> http://employers.commuterlink.com/incentives.php

20. **North Carolina Recycling Business Development Grants**
    The Recycling Business Assistance Center aims to encourage sustainability and reduce waste with this yearly grant program.
    - **Visit HERE:**
      https://deq.nc.gov/conservation/recycling-business-assistance/financing/grants

21. **North Carolina IDEA**
    NC IDEA gives out grants of up to $50,000 and has sponsored nearly 100 high-tech companies with growth potential. This is actually a private foundation, but their grants are open only to North Carolina businesses. There are different grants for different types of companies—such as women-owned businesses or seed-stage businesses.
    - **Visit HERE: http://ncidea.org/grants-programs/**

22. **Tennessee Department of Economic & Community Development**
    With small business grants for companies that are expanding, offering training initiatives, or improving public infrastructure, the Tennessee DOECD isn't one to skip if you're located in the right place.
    - **Visit HERE:**
      https://www.tnecd.com/advantages/incentives-grants/

23. **Texas Young Farmer Grant**
    For residents between 18 and 46 years of age, this
    grant funds projects that support Texas' agricultural
    production and community.
    - **Visit HERE:**
      http://www.texasagriculture.gov/GrantsServices/Rur
      alEconomicDevelopment/TexasAgriculturalFinanceA
      uthority/YoungFarmerGrant.aspx

SMALL BUSINESS GRANTS: LOCAL

In addition to statewide grants, cities, towns, and nonprofits
finance their own small business grant programs. For local small
business grants, you've got a substantial upper hand if you
service your community in a tangible and demonstrable way.

Plus, is your small business aimed at promoting health,
environmental consciousness, or similar initiatives? If so, you'll
be looking at even more local grants to apply for—and get
funding from. Because local small business grants are so
geographically specific, I have pulled just a few to show you
what kinds of opportunities may exist in your nearby city or
town.

- **Note: Make sure to look for similar programs in your
  own locality.**

1. **Cleveland Department of Economic Development**
   Many cities—including Cleveland, which we'll use as an example for this section—will have a number of small business grants and initiatives to foster entrepreneurship.
   - **Visit HERE:**
     http://rethinkcleveland.org/About-Us/Our-Programs.aspx

2. **Green Technology Business Grant Program**
   Environmental sustainability initiatives exist at every level of the government, so consider going green to save with your small business.
   - **Visit HERE:**
     http://rethinkcleveland.org/About-Us/Our-Programs/Green-Technology-Business-Grant-Program.aspx

3. **Ben Franklin Technology Partners**
   Big Idea Contest Continuing the trend of encouraging research and development, contest presented a challenge to companies in Central and Northern Pennsylvania and awarded a sizeable grant—alongside $50,000 in cash, a $100,000 low-interest loan, special service access and consultation.
   - **Visit HERE:**
     http://cnp.benfranklin.org/big-idea-contest/

4. **Ben Franklin Innovation Partnership**
   The Ben Franklin Technology Partnership partially funds the Innovation Partnership, which is a local grant program centered around helping Pennsylvanian small businesses afford those SBIR and STTR Federal research and development grant programs we looked at way back when. Though this is statewide, we're including it under the local category because it's actually a consolidation of microloan programs throughout the region.
   - **Visit HERE: https://innovationpartnership.net/**

5. **Chicago IncentOvate**
   In past years, this project has awarded $400,000 to cultural projects in the city of Chicago. While it's unclear whether this grant will be repeated in future years, it's a reflection of grants you should be looking for in your own city! You don't need to be running a research and development business or a green technology-oriented farm to get small business grants, after all.
   - **Visit HERE:**
     https://www.cityofchicago.org/city/en/depts/dca/prov drs/grants/news/2015/november/incentovate.html

6. **Chicago Small Business Improvement Fund**
   The SBIF supports small businesses repairing or
   remodeling their location, whether by updating windows
   and floors, replacing signage, or purchasing nearby
   property to expand into. Note that you'd receive this
   matching grant after completing and paying for your
   remodeling, so be cautious—plenty of other businesses
   are likely competing for small business grants like these.
   • **Visit HERE:**
     **https://www.cityofchicago.org/city/en/depts/dcd/supp
     _info/small_business_improvementfundsbif.html**

7. **Miami Mom & Pop Small Business Grant**
   If you're in Miami and have been in business for at least
   a year, make sure to apply to this program meant to
   "bridge the gap between local government and small
   owned and operated businesses."
   • **Visit HERE:**
     **https://www8.miamidade.gov/global/service.page?Md
     uid_service=ser1471548035447835&Mduid_location=
     org1462994438372631&Type_collection=&Mduid_or
     ganization=org1462994438372631**

8. **New York City Fashion Manufacturing Initiative**
   The FMI offers grants to New York City fashion
   companies who need to purchase equipment, make
   upgrades, or train their employees.
   • **Visit HERE:**
     **https://www.nycedc.com/program/fashion-
     manufacturing-initiative-fmi**

9. **New York City Job Creation and Retention Program**
   Is your small business new to Lower Manhattan, and can you commit to creating at least 75 new jobs in the area? If so, look to the JCRP grant.
   - **Visit HERE: https://www.nycedc.com/program/job-creation-and-retention-program**

10. **Lumpkin Foundation Grant**
    The Lumpkin Foundation is a private foundation, but they provide grants to organizations in East Central Illinois. Grants are available to businesses that focus on food service, the local agriculture economy, and sustainable practices.
    - **Visit HERE: https://www.lumpkinfoundation.org/for-grant-seekers/Land-Health-Community**

11. **Orlando Downtown Facade & Building Stabilization Program**
    This program provides grants between $5,000 and $40,000 to small businesses that own their buildings in downtown Orlando and improve their stability or appearance. Part infrastructural, part city beautification, this program incentivizes the small business owning residents of Orlando to contribute to their city's well-being in a few different ways.
    - **Visit HERE: http://www.downtownorlando.com/ business/business-incentives/#.W8bRIGhKjIW**

12. **Detroit NEIdeas**

   Grants Aimed at fostering economic growth and entrepreneurial spirit in Detroit (alongside a few other cities), the NEIdeas grant program gives out $10,000 and $100,000 grants to businesses—as well as exposure and free resources.

   - **Visit HERE: https://neideasdetroit.org/guidelines/rules-eligibility/**

13. **Roseburg, Oregon Tourism Grant**

   Local townships and cities, as well as states, give tourism grants to businesses that promote travel. This particular grant also weighs whether your business is promoting tourism during season or off-season, which is something to consider.

   - **Visit HERE: http://www.cityofroseburg.org/doing-business/economic-development/**

14. **Salt Lake City River District Gardens Facade Improvement Grant**

   Part of a local beautification program, this grant applies only to businesses within a certain district of the city. Again, though not a lot of money, small business grants like these are uncompetitive and low in effort to apply for—who's going to turn down free cash?

   - **Visit HERE: https://www.slc.gov/ed/**

15. **San Francisco Historic Preservation Grant**
The city of San Francisco gives grants and business loans for emerging and established businesses. Grants are available to companies that are working on preserving and rehabilitating historic buildings. This could be perfect for retail, brick and mortar businesses.
- **Visit HERE: https://oewd.org/grant-and-loan-programs**

**Recommended: Job Creation Tax Abatements
Your small business might be in an Enterprise Zone (as Ohio terms it), or a similar type of area, and accordingly be offered tax incentives for projects or operations that create jobs. These aren't technically small business grants, but they put additional money in your business's pocket that you can use to grow.
- **Visit HERE: http://rethinkcleveland.org/About-Us/Our-Programs/Enterprise-Zone-Tax-Abatement.aspx**

**Recommended: Seed Chicago
Seed Chicago is a crowdfunding platform specifically for Chicago-based businesses. This is technically not a small business grant, but crowdfunding is money which comes from many different community backers. In most cases, you don't have to pay back the money.
- **Visit HERE:
https://us.accion.org/resource/seedchicago/**

SMALL BUSINESS GRANTS: CORPORATE

Government grants are great, but the requirements are often hyper-specific, or the funding amounts aren't that large. Big corporations will often provide small business grants to contest winners. For you, it's money to grow your business. For them, it's a PR win, netting loyal corporate customers and a lot of good will.

The difference here is that many corporate-sponsored small business grants involve pitch competitions or something similar. Not all do, of course, but you'll want to be aware that applying to a corporate grant might involve more work.

- **Note: These grants come with the potential for publicity that can bring exposure to your business—and for runner-up prizes. Publicity always a plus!**

1. **Intuit National Association for the Self-Employed (NASE) Grant**
   Intuit, the tax preparation software company, gives small businesses a $4,000 grant in partnership with NASE. This is designed to help small businesses and freelancers take their business to the next level. Although the application period ended last year, Intuit usually gives out small business grants annually.
- **Visit HERE: https://www.nase.org/become-a-member/member-benefits/business-resources/growth-grants**

2. **FedEx Small Business Grant**
   FedEx annually awards grants of up to $25,000 to ten small businesses, nationwide, with its Small Business Grant Contest. You can check out past winners—and hear their words of wisdom and warning—and the FedEx site.
   - **Visit HERE:**
     https://smallbusiness.fedex.com/grant-contest

3. **Etsy Maker Cities Grant**
   If you're a maker of furniture, crafts, ceramics, fabrics, art—or anything else that Etsy sellers offer—then check out their small business grant contest. Called Maker Cities, only non-profits and educational institutions are eligible. However, those recipients support small business. This is a great way to get more vintage and handmade goods into the hands of customers.
   - **Visit HERE:**
     https://www.etsy.com/seller-handbook/article/apply-to-etsys-maker-cities-grant/111850053574

4. **Chase Mission Main Street Grants**
   Each year, Chase Bank puts aside $3 million to split between 20 small businesses—that's $150,000 each. You'll have to answer a few essay questions regarding your business, its story, and its community impact, and then winners are decided by a panel of small business experts and senior executives. You'll also get a free trip to Google for a small business marketing workshop, and more.
   - **Visit HERE:**
     https://www.jpmorganchase.com/corporate/news/stories/mission-main-street-grants.htm

5. **Visa Everywhere Initiative**
   Visa's Everywhere Initiative looks for startups with innovative fixes and offered $50,000 to the final three winners.
   - **Visit HERE: https://usa.visa.com/visa-everywhere/everywhere-initiative/initiative.html**

6. **Marriott International's Canvas**
   Canvas is a "food and drink concept lab" maintained by Marriott International—so if you're an aspiring restaurateur in need of money, space, or advice, look no further. Unlike many small business grants, this funding opportunity is for the concept stage only.
   - **Visit HERE: http://www.canvas-startup.com/**

7. **Sam's Club Grant Program**
   Now, this grant program doesn't directly assist small businesses—instead, it offers funding to nonprofit organizations that support small business owners. So while you can't apply, you should keep tabs on the program and its recipients, in case any wind up in your neck of the woods.
   - **Visit HERE: http://giving.walmart.com/sams-club-grant-program**

8. **Wells Fargo Community Investment**
   Offering grants in nearly every state, the Wells Fargo Community Investment program focuses mainly on nonprofits—but small businesses with the right criteria can qualify, too.
   - **Visit HERE: https://www.wellsfargo.com/about/corporate-responsibility/community-giving/**

9. **Wal-Mart Foundation**
   Wal-Mart has a number of different grant programs, again mostly aimed towards nonprofits. Similar to the Sam's Club program, you should apply if you can, but keep tabs on relevant nonprofits who might want to sponsor you in turn.
   - **Visit HERE: http://giving.walmart.com/foundation**

10. **ExxonMobile Foundation**
    This philanthropic arm of Exxon Mobile focuses on funding sources concerned with eliminating malaria, increasing math and science education, and investing in women's economic opportunities.
    - **Visit HERE: https://corporate.exxonmobil.com/en/community/worldwide-giving/exxonmobil-foundation/overview**

11. **Coca-Cola Foundation**
    Similarly, Coca-Cola's community-giving branch centers around empowering women, improving access to clean water, and fostering healthy living and youth development. If your small business doesn't qualify under the mostly charity-centric criteria, then try to see if you can contract or cater for the nonprofit that does.
    - **Visit HERE: https://www.coca-colacompany.com/our-company/the-coca-cola-foundation**

12. **National Association for the Self-Employed**
    NASE offers small business grants of up to $5,000. Just register and see if you're eligible! Some of these grants, mentioned above, are in conjunction with Intuit.
    - **Visit HERE:**
      https://www.nase.org/become-a-member/grants-and-scholarships/BusinessDevelopmentGrants.aspx

13. **LendingTree**
    2017 was the inaugural year for LendingTree's Small Business Grant Contest. The winning small business will receive $50,000 to fund the needs of their growing business!
    - **Visit HERE:**
      https://www.lendingtree.com/business/grant/

SMALL BUSINESS GRANTS FOR WOMEN

There are many Federal, State, Local, and Corporate initiatives that offer money to female entrepreneurs, in order to work towards fixing the gender gap and promoting equality in business.

1. **Eileen Fisher Program**
   Awarding $100,000 in grant money to up to 10 recipients, initiative is geared towards small businesses interested in creating environmental and social change—and, of course, companies owned and run by women.
   - **Visit HERE:**
     https://www.eileenfisher.com/grants/women-owned-business/women-owned-business-overview/

2. **Zions Bank Smart Women Grants**
    Zions Bank offers $18,000 across six categories, including child and elder care, arts and culture, and teacher support.
    - **Visit HERE: https://www.zionsbank.com/business-banking/small-business-resources/**

3. **The Amber Grant**
    With a number of different grant initiatives for women, WomensNet Amber Grant program is a great place to look for assistance with your business, especially at an early stage.
    - **Visit HERE: https://ambergrantsforwomen.com/get-an-amber-grant/**

4. **American Association of University Women Career Development Grant**
    If you're a woman who holds a B.A. and is looking to advance or change careers, the AAUW's career development program can help you fund that major life shift.
    - **Visit HERE: https://www.aauw.org/what-we-do/educational-funding-and-awards/career-development-grants/**

5. **Open Meadows Foundation**
    Open Meadows funds projects with $2,000 grants, as long as they're designed and led by women. The projects should also aid racial, gender, and economic justice.
    - **Visit HERE: https://sites.google.com/site/openmeadowsfoundation/**

6. **The Halstead Grant**
   This funding opportunity is for business owners who make and sell jewelry. Although open to men, women tend to be much more active in this industry. You'll receive $7,500 in cash, a $1,000 gift certificate to Halstead, and a variety of social media and public relations spotlights—as well as a trip to Arizona. The top ten runners-up receive prizes as well, so don't let anything hold you back from entering!
   - **Visit HERE:**
     https://grant.halsteadbead.com/Application/

7. **Idea Cafe Grant**
   This program gives women $1,000 micro-grants to start or grow a business. Again, men are free to apply for this grant, but most of the former winners have been women.
   - **Visit HERE:**
     https://www.businessownersideacafe.com/small_busi ness_grants/index.php

   **Recommended: Women's Business Centers
   This isn't a direct grant provider, but rather a database of Small Business Administration-sponsored Women's Business Centers. Some centers give out small business grants themselves, while others will simply help you find local corporations or foundations that do so. Either way, make sure to check yours out.
   - **Visit HERE:**
     https://www.sba.gov/tools/local-assistance/wbc

**Recommended: Walmart Global Women's Economic Empowerment Initiative
Though an international program, Walmart's GWEEI should still be on your list if you're a female business owner: they've pledged to support women-owned businesses with over $100 million in grants. Although a lot of this money goes to overseas businesses, some is reserved for women-owned businesses in the US.

- **Visit HERE: https://www.zionsbank.com/business-banking/small-business-resources/**

SMALL BUSINESS GRANTS FOR MINORITIES

In a similar vein, these small business grants are intended to help minority business owners overcome the unique social, political, and economic challenges they've historically faced.

Many governmental grant programs focus on businesses owned by individuals who belong to a Federally-recognized Native American tribe.

- **Note: Even if these grants are for a community rather than a small business, check with the grantor to see if they'll make an exception.**

Grant seeking requires creativity, determination, and patience—so don't be afraid to think outside of the box.

1. **Minerals and Mining on Indian Lands**
   This Department of the Interiors grant provides funding to both tribes and individual mineral owners seeking to make use of those resources on Indian lands.
   - **Visit HERE:**
     https://www.federalgrantswire.com/minerals-and-mining-on-indian-lands.html#.W8bdHmhKjIV

2. **Empowered Communities for a Healthier Nation Initiative**
   If you own a health-related small business, you can use this grant to spread information and awareness of health and healthcare for minorities.
   - **Visit HERE:**
     https://minorityhealth.hhs.gov/omh/browse.aspx?lvl=1&lvlid=5

3. **POWER**
   President Obama began the Partnerships for Opportunity, Workforce, and Economic Revitalization Initiative to help communities hurt by the changing power industry. Look into the block grants the federal government awarded to state and local institutions, and if you're nearby, see if you can snag a contracting opportunity or second-hand grant from them.
   - **Visit HERE:**
     https://obamawhitehouse.archives.gov/the-press-office/2015/03/27/fact-sheet-partnerships-opportunity-and-workforce-and-economic-revitaliz

4. **Rural Business Enterprise Grants**
   Available to small businesses, the RBEG program offers funds for rural development—including, by not limited to, infrastructural development, working capital for startup businesses, purchasing equipment, and real estate development. Smaller requests are actually given higher priority, and grants usually range between $10,000 and $50,000. Federally recognized Indian tribes are among the eligible applicants.
   - **Visit HERE:**
     https://www.rd.usda.gov/programs-services/rural-business-development-grants

5. **Community Connect Grants**
   If you live or operate in a rural area that lacks an Internet broadband speed of 3 Mbps or more, and are looking to fix that, then check to see whether you're eligible for this Department of Agriculture grant. Indian tribes are also a major target demographic for these programs.
   - **Visit HERE:**
     https://www.rd.usda.gov/programs-services/community-connect-grants

6. **Water & Waste Disposal Loan & Grant Program**
Though not explicitly targeted towards small businesses, this grant initiative—like many others—includes Federally-recognized tribes among its eligible applicants. If you're a business owner operating in recognized tribal lands, and you'd like to invest in water or waste disposal, this cash could help out.
- **Visit HERE: https://www.rd.usda.gov/programs-services/water-waste-disposal-loan-grant-program**

7. **Minority Business Development Agency**
The MBDA has regular grant competitions for minority business owners, alongside a long list of other resources for you to learn from.
- **Visit HERE: https://www.mbda.gov/page/grants-and-loans**

8. **First Nations Development Institute Grant**
The Native Arts Capacity Building Initiative gives up to six grants of $30,000 each to Native American institutions supporting arts and culture. However, to qualify you must already have programs in place supporting this goal. The program is limited to those initiatives that support Native American artists in Minnesota, North Dakota, south Dakota, and Wisconsin.
- **Visit HERE: https://firstnations.org/grantmaking**

9. **Tribal Energy Development Capacity Grant**
   This program gives Federally-recognized tribes more resources to improve the economic influence of energy development in their areas. While this grant doesn't provide directly to small businesses, look for the "trickle down" approach of funneling this government money into your business by securing the right contracts.
   - **Visit HERE: https://www.bia.gov/as-ia/ieed/division-energy-and-mineral-development/tedcp**

**Recommended: Small Business Administration 8(a) Certification Program This program is not a grant— however, it is a federally-funded initiative aimed towards helping minority-owned small businesses capture more clients and work, so I decided to include it.

- **The SBA's 8(a) program guarantees minority-owned businesses special government contracts that they might otherwise not have access to.**

SMALL BUSINESS GRANTS FOR VETERANS

Finally, veteran-owned businesses are eligible to receive certain small business grants from the government, nonprofits, and some corporations as well.

I was tired of seeing our troops homeless after their service to America. So, I did some research and compile a list of grants to help ANY veterans out there who is reading 30 Days 50K book.

These initiatives seek to give back to our troops for their service and dedication, and to support their entrepreneurial contributions.

1. **StreetShares Commander's Call Veteran Business Award**
   This program rewards veterans or military spouses who run businesses with up to $15,000 in grant money.
   - **Visit HERE: http://go.streetshares.com/streetshares-foundation-veteran-small-business-award**

2. **USDA Veteran and Minority Farmer Grant**
   The 2501 Program, run by the Department of Agriculture, gives small business grants—as well as education, training, outreach, and other forms of support—to veterans and minorities looking to begin or expand their agricultural operations.
   - **Visit HERE: https://www.outreach.usda.gov/grants/index.htm**

**Recommended: Service Disabled Veteran-Owned Small Businesses Program
Similar to the 8(a) program, the SBA's SDVOSBP isn't a grant, but it helps veterans who own businesses get additional contracting opportunities from the government.

- **Visit HERE: https://www.sba.gov/federal-contracting/contracting-assistance-programs/service-disabled-veteran-owned-small-businesses-program**

**Note: Small Business Administration Veteran's Entrepreneurship Act of 2015-- The SBA's Veteran Entrepreneurship Act removes the borrower fee on Express Loans of up to $350,000 awarded to veteran-owned businesses.

Removing the fee makes the SBA loans more affordable for veterans.
- **Visit HERE:**
  https://www.sba.gov/document/information-notice-5000-1356-veterans-entrepreneurship-act-2015-fee-relief-veterans-and-credit-elsewhere

**Recommended: UPS Franchise Discount
While not quite a grant, this initiative gives veterans looking to join the UPS franchise a $10,000 discount off the franchise fee, and 50-75%% off the initial application fee. The UPS Store ranked as the top participant of the Veterans Transition Franchise Initiative program in 2008 and has a large number of its locations run by veteran entrepreneurs.
- **Visit HERE:**
  https://www.theupsstorefranchise.com/opportunities

**Recommended: 7-Eleven Veterans Franchising
Similar to UPS and a number of other companies, 7-Eleven offers special benefits to veteran franchisees. If you're eligible, you can receive up to 20% off the initial franchise fee, up to 65% financing through 7-Eleven, and special financing options.
- **Visit HERE:**
  http://franchise.7-eleven.com/franchise/franchises-for-veterans-program

**Recommended: Little Caesars Veterans Program
As you've seen by now, if you're a veteran looking to start your own business, franchising could be a worthwhile path to pursue. Little Caesars Pizza offers a set of discounts to honorably discharged veterans, including a $5,000 franchise fee discount, the same amount off the first equipment order, and other marketing and supply services that total up to $30,000. Service-disabled veterans qualify for even more, including a full waiver of the full $20,000 franchise fee and $30,000 worth of other benefits.

- **Visit HERE: https://franchise.littlecaesars.com/ VeteransProgram.aspx**

SMALL BUSINESS GRANTS FOR STARTUPS

Many small business grants are open only to businesses that have been operating for a few years and have an established product or service.

However, it's often the newest businesses that need the most financial assistance.

1. **A Grant for Greatness**
   Hosted by AT&T Experts, this grant offers $1,000 to unique business ideas submitted in the form of a two-minute video. (Note that if your business is already established, annual revenue can't be greater than $20,000).
- **Visit HERE: https://www.attexperts.com/grant**

2. **ActivityHero Business Grant**
    Co-sponsored by web hosting service GoDaddy, this grant awards cash and prizes (worth $15,000) to 9 Kid's Camp and Activity Providers to grow their businesses. To win, fill out an application, get 3 family reviews, and boost your odds with votes from customers!
    - **Visit HERE: https://camps.activityhero.com/2018-business-grant-contest/**

3. **Fundera's Zach Grant**
    Fundera now hosts their very own small business grant, giving out $2,500 every year to entrepreneurs looking to start or fund their businesses. All you have to do is submit a video entry to the annual contest explaining why you started your company, follow us on social media, and… That's all! Apply to get that easy capital.
    - **Visit HERE: https://www.fundera.com/resources/zach-grant**

Small Business Grants Are a Great Option to get funding for your business while building your business credit.

Small business grants mean free money in your pocket, so if you're able to qualify for one, congratulations!

These grants will help you along your business's journey. There are grants for startups, as well as established companies, but if a grant doesn't work out for you, don't let that hold you back.

Other financing options can work within your budget like those mentioned in this book. I wrote 30 Days 50K book to help business owners and individuals looking to receive funding for ANY type of business.

I did all the research for you and I used these exact tricks and tips to grow my own empire.

**Recommended: There is also a service called Instrumentl that finds grants for your business. You can think of Instrumentl as your automated grant assistant that saves you time and broadens your funding sources with a refreshingly intuitive online platform.

Once you set up your projects, they do the legwork to match you with relevant grants. All of the grants you are matched with are active funding opportunities with upcoming deadlines.

Instrumentl pulls from corporate, private, federal, and even state funding sources so you don't have to search anywhere else. Instrumentl is bringing in new funding opportunities daily so you always have the latest information at your fingertips.

Instrumentl also has a built-in project management tool called the Grant Tracker that you can use to save your favorite grants, receive deadline reminders, track your progress, and even store notes & documents.

- Visit HERE: https://www.instrumentl.com/

RECAP: Remember that even if you have bad personal credit you are STILL able to get a business line of credit by fixing your credit score with Authorized Users, Primary Tradelines mentioned on Page 23 and 25.

Thanks again for your support and I hope to hear from you in the future about all your business success. My contact information is listed in page 92. Please leave a review of what you thank about 30 Days 50K book at www.30days50k.com and All major book stores where 30 Days 50K book is sold. I also have book promo t-shirts available for Entrepreneurs worldwide.

Thank You's

I have to give a special thanks to my friends and my best title closing agent Stephanie Rosario, and my "lil bro" Harold Pompee, can't wait till I see you again.

God used my first-born son Ian Pompee to push me back into my purpose.

To do what I do best!

Special, special thanks to the whole Pompee Family, my mom Rose Marie Pompee, you are always there for me and I love you forever to my sister Fabianne Pompee and her son Dishon Smith and her newborn twins coming to this world at the end of this year 2018 and To my Wife Nefertiti Pompee, you're my backbone and to her family, and to her mom, you are a wonderful mom, and many, many more who saw something in me, supported me, or gave me a chance when no one else would. Thank you all!

ABOUT THE AUTHOR

Self-taught on investing in his early 20's, Garry Frantz Pompee nationally recognized for his Business Management Success and lifestyle transformation. His Real Estate ventures have been very successful, earning Garry Thousands in revenue to date. As a Founder and CEO of Happie Monsters, Inc. a baby product corporation, Garry also educates new investors how to run a successful ecommerce business on Amazon FBA, helps first time home buyers get approved, and mentors the youth nationwide how to trade stocks and making smart investments. Garry currently provides Business Management Services that helped many business owners grow their company. He also teaches how to wholesale real estate with NO LICENSE AND NO CASH NEEDED at Prestige Elite Group. Their offices are in the most affluent areas of the US. With his persistence, intelligence, and Business Credit prowess, Garry has built a life style for himself with millionaire clientele. Garry PASSION is educating and inspiring the youth, especially those who need it the most!

AN ESSENTIAL FOR SUCCESS

Arthur: Garry Pompee
Published By: Prestige Elite Group
"An Essential for Success"
www.prestigeelitegroup.com
Facebook: @prestigeelitegroup
Twitter: @prestigeelitegp
Instagram: @prestigeelitegroupllc
4181 NW 1st Ave, Boca Raton FL 33431
1-800-992-6163
support@prestigeelitegroup.com
Business Financial Suite
www.businessfinancialsuite.com
Founder/CEO Happie Monsters, Inc.
"All Things Baby"
www.happiemonsters.com
30 Days 50K
www.30days50k.com